T0207621

WHERE DO YOU *Kneel?*

BURT PALMER

WESTBOW
PRESS®
A DIVISION OF THOMAS NELSON
& ZONDERVAN

WestBow Press books may be ordered through booksellers or by contacting:

WestBow Press
A Division of Thomas Nelson & Zondervan
1663 Liberty Drive
Bloomington, IN 47403
www.westbowpress.com
1 (866) 928-1240

ISBN: 978-1-5127-0523-2 (sc)
ISBN: 978-1-5127-0522-5 (e)

Library of Congress Control Number: 2015911942

Print information available on the last page.

WestBow Press rev. date: 11/17/2015

Contents

The people all said to Samuel,
"Pray to the LORD
your God for your servants
so that we will not die,
for we have added to all our other sins
the evil of asking for a king."
"Do not be afraid," Samuel replied.
"You have done all this evil;
yet do not turn away from the LORD,
but serve the LORD with all your heart.
Do not turn away after useless idols.
They can do you no good,
nor can they rescue you,
because they are useless.
For the sake of
his great name
the LORD
will not reject his people,
because the LORD
was pleased
to make you his own."
(1 Sam. 12:19–22 NIV)

Introduction

First Samuel records the relationship between God and his people, which Samuel, one of the last prophetic judges of Israel, mediates. It is about Samuel's journey as he leads God's people through difficult times of faithfulness. The people seem consumed not only with a memory of what their God has done for them but also of wanting something else—something that will alleviate their struggles. Samuel listens to the people's pleas. He presents these pleas to the Lord. With a divine consent, the Lord instructs Samuel to give the people what they are longing for.

> But the people refused to listen to Samuel. "No!" they said. "We want a king over us. Then we will be like all the other nations, with a king to lead us and to *go out before us and fight our battles*." When Samuel heard all that the people said, he repeated it before the LORD. The LORD answered, "Listen to them and give them a king." (1 Sam. 8:19–22 NIV, emphasis added)

Several chapters later, Samuel confronts the Israelites with their rebellion against God's purposes. The people repentantly acknowledge that by demanding a king, they have sinned.

> The people all said to Samuel, "Pray to the LORD your God for your servants so that we will not die, for we have added to all our other sins the evil of asking for a king." "Do not be afraid," Samuel replied. "You have done all this evil; yet do not turn away from the LORD, but serve the LORD with all your heart. Do not turn away after useless idols. They can do you no good, nor can they rescue you, because they are useless. For the sake of his great name the LORD will not reject his people, because the LORD was pleased to make you his own." (1 Sam. 12:19–22 NIV, emphasis added)

The people are so convinced and convicted of their sin, they plead to Samuel, "Pray to the LORD *your* God" (verse 19). Though the God of Abraham and Sarah never ceased being their God, the people imagine that their sin of demanding a king has alienated them from God. Instead of adding to their guilt by driving home the point that they have sinned, Samuel comforts them with words of instruction, encouragement, and hope.

Samuel specifically links their desire for a king to the worship of idols. He knows this desire is really about their belief that if they have what others possess, all their struggles will be alleviated. Samuel's earlier attempts to help the people understand this would not alleviate their struggles seemed futile. But now the people are hungry to be faithful. As the people begin their earnest journey to become authentically faithful to God, Samuel gives this added word of instruction, "Do not turn away after useless idols. They can do you no good, nor can they rescue you, because they are useless" (verse 21). And it is a word that useless idols can do us no good nor rescue us is a word we need to hear today.

How often are we distracted from seeing God's involvement in our lives? How often do we forget the divine that exists in the ordinary and turn away from the sacred that is present in the simple to pursue modern idols—idols that would certainly alleviate our struggles and fight our battles for us? These modern idols are seductive. They are ideals that, in and of themselves, are not innately evil. However, when we pursue or worship them in a manner that replaces the worship of God, we transform them into idols. We exchange our faith and trust in God for a hope and trust in something else.

In the late sixth century, Pope Gregory the Great was the first to articulate what we know as the seven deadly sins: pride, envy, anger, greed, sadness (which later became sloth or laziness), gluttony, and lust. History has illustrated how the church has both abused these principles and utilized them for good through the disciplines of the Christian faith. But in our world today, with all of our perceived advances in technology, education, research, communication, and medicine, our great struggle is with these four modern idols:

Novelty
Structure
Destination
Answers

Each of these concepts, in and of themselves, is not destructive and actually possesses critical components that are vital to healthy living. However, when any one of these concepts becomes the sole goal and aim of the Christian life, the concept actually becomes an idol. The idolatry happens when we believe that Novelty (something new), Structure (the right organizational format), Destination (getting to the right place in your job or life), or Answers (having the correct information) will, in essence, *fight our battles for us*. This kind of idolatry is the underlying motivation expressed by the proverbial phrase, "The grass is always greener on the other side" of the fence.

Join me on a journey to explore *Where Do You Kneel?* As you do, your modern ideologies of God's creation and God's Word will be challenged. You will hear ancient words of faith like those Samuel spoke so long ago.

> They [idols] can do you no good, nor can they rescue you, because they are useless. For the sake of his great name the LORD will not reject his people, because the LORD was pleased to make you his own. (1 Sam. 12:21–22 NIV)

It is good news to hear that the Lord still wants to make us his own, regardless of where we have been or the mistakes we have made. God is always willing to forgive and receive us, but we are the ones who must be willing to stop following the things that lead us away from God and to turn toward God. Like the father of the Prodigal Son in the Gospel of Luke, God rejoices when we come home to him.

Preface

I have always enjoyed the game of golf. I can remember growing up near Northwood Country Club in Dallas and playing four holes of golf with my dad. I toted a "little Ben" five-iron around in a canvas bag. I'd play those four holes and then jump in the pool while my dad finished his round of golf. As time went by, I stretched the number of holes I could play and probably stretched the patience and love of my dad when I couldn't keep my temper during those teenage years.

In the summer months of my junior and senior years of high school, I played at the Wichita Falls Country Club. I can fondly remember the lazy, hot, summer evenings when Dad and I would walk nine holes just before dark. Whenever my mother joined us, she found a way to win. She would say, "We're playing for who does the dishes tonight," and then would define the battlefield clearly, saying, "Whoever has the fewest putts doesn't have to do the dishes." What I didn't know then was my mom's strategy. On the par-3 ninth hole, when I'd step up and hit an iron to the green, I'd be arrogantly proud of my accomplishment. Mom, on the other hand, would chunk a seven-wood down toward the green and then play a seven-iron short of the green. By now, she would be hitting her third shot, but still not on the green. She'd chip up within a few feet of the hole and one putt. I've seen her play around sand traps before getting onto the green. She could record eight strokes on the hole but still win because she made the rules. Remember, mom said the winner wasn't the one with the fewest number of strokes on the hole, it was the one with the fewest number of putts that won. What I really learned from my mother was how to make myself competitive and how to win—something she does in every part of her life—just ask my dad!

This book is really about getting to know yourself. Golf is just one tool that allows me to reflect on my life without becoming too defensive. It helps me ask challenging questions. It shows me how aware I am of my actions in my personal walk with Christ, in my involvement in my faith community, and in my leadership. Most importantly, golf lifts up one of the hardest realities to embrace in life and leadership, the golf ball doesn't go anywhere by itself. My mom and dad have helped me see that in so many ways. I took the love of golf with me through college, graduate school, and even love it today.

I was appointed to Calvary United Methodist Church in Paris, Texas, in June 2001. Shortly after arriving in Paris, I learned a valuable lesson that has been both the catalyst and genesis for this work. I was invited to my inaugural Sunday afternoon golf outing with the guys at church. The group had a spectacular combination of characters and abilities: Bob was the in choir and worked part time with the Lamar County Sheriff's Department; Alan was our anal-retentive rules man and had a temper; Nick was a senior at Paris High School and could hit a five-iron as far as most of us could drive the ball; Nick's dad, Jay, was a radiologist at the hospital; and Larry made glasses.

I was paired up with Larry, who was the husband of an associate pastor at Calvary United Methodist Church. I did the normally gracious thing any golfer would do—checked out his bag and clubs without him knowing it. What I learned, while living in a suburb of Dallas, was the equipment you had and how you looked were important to the game. Don't tell Larry this, but I thought he'd be hitting last most of the afternoon. (In golf, the one who finishes with the highest score on a hole tees off last at the next hole).

Larry's clubs were old. His bag looked like it was rejected from a yard sale—it was plastic, the metal parts were rusted, and the strap looked like it was drug underneath a golf cart a few too many times. Larry's bag didn't have club head covers. His shoes were not shined. This guy didn't look like a golfer. He had a pipe that he stuffed with fresh tobacco. His long hair blew in the breeze, but at least he didn't have it in a ponytail. In golf, the person who has the most number of strokes on the previous hole will tee off last. The only time Larry hit last was on the first hole.

I teed off last a couple of times, and so did everybody but Nick. I realized that I had wrongly assumed that Larry's ability to play golf was related to what I thought of him and his appearance. Larry shot an even round of golf that day. I did not. Larry understood his game and focused on doing what he knew he could. I tried to cut corners and do things I watched the pros do.

I made an incorrect assumption that day because of the false ideas I had adopted. I thought that having shoes, a golf bag, and clubs with logos would make me a better golfer. Until that day, I hadn't realized I was being arrogant and thinking erroneously. I put the things that mattered least—the tools—first and the thing that mattered most—the basics of the game—last.

How do we put the least important thing first? We hear something is new and "better than ever" or "never before been used" and unquestionably adopt this new idea. We read about a structural or organizational format that should magically remove all of our problems, and we duplicate it without another thought. We struggle through life and want answers, yet too often, we accept, without any challenge, a set of answers that we repeatedly apply to any situation and effectively surrender our spirit and intellect to the world. We believe that if we can just get to that "next"—the thing that clearly says you have arrived, such as the right job, the right house in the right location, and the right car—we won't have any more problems.

In these very subtle ways, we kneel at the altar of novelty, structure, destination, and answers. Until some life altering event reveals that we have allowed our faith in God to be replaced by these idolatrous ideas, we're stuck in that place.

How do we kneel before God and not before idols? The last chapter of this book, "Defining Your Dash," is about finding balance in your life. We must learn how to live a faith that knows the distinction between faithful determination that endures and self-absorbed illusions. We find that distinction in community with others who are willing to be honest and vulnerable. We need a community of faith where we can be challenged, affirmed, and supported in our Christian walk with Christ. I have experienced this myself. When I am alone and pray to God, God tends to always agree with me; however, when I pray to God with my brothers and sisters in the faith, God doesn't always agree with me.

Chapter 1

NOVELTY

Novelty is defined by The Free Dictionary as, "(1) the quality of being novel; newness; or (2) something new and unusual; an innovation."

Novelty becomes an idol when we believe that something will fight all of our battles for us because it is new. We are lured into novelty and allow it to become an idol when we place our trust and belief in its newness to alleviate our struggles. We falsely believe that the latest revelation of ideas will become revolutionary in our lives. At the very least, we begin to have faith in the "newest revelation" and miss the larger context of life. At the very worst, we believe that salvation rests in the most recent idea.

While I believe that the following examples have blessed the lives of many people and were never intended to replace the primacy of biblical witness, when we incorporate them into our lives, we can move these tremendous ideas from a place of *supporting* the Christian walk to the *replacing* of faith altogether. If one considers the *Prayer of Jabez* rage or the *Forty Days of Purpose* program, both of them were novel when introduced and were worthy contributions to our faith—until the new ideas or programs became God. This idol placement occurs when we allow any particular program to be our answer or the lens of the newest idea to be the only perspective through which we view our Christian reality. When we view our Christian reality through anything less than the life, death, and resurrection of Jesus Christ, we have made that idea our idol.

On the other extreme, declaring new ideas or perspectives on the Christian reality as evil, simply because they are new, is also a form of idolatry. This occurs when we don't even consider the concept or idea because we've never done it that way before. When any new idea is seen, in and of itself, as evil, we become unchanging and stagnant.

While growing up in Wichita Falls, Texas, I'd see the occasional spring rain cause the creeks to swell above their banks and create ponds out of low lying areas. Approaching summer, as the temperatures began to rise, those stagnant waters would reek of a foul smell. I can attest to the fact that stagnant waters do not breed life that can be sustained—they simply evaporate or decay matter. When we become so reactionary and rigid we do not allow anything new to penetrate our lives, we are in that same decaying process. I think this was the very struggle Jesus confronted throughout his ministry and that is most clearly observed in his teaching in the synagogue.

> He went to Nazareth, where he had been brought up, and on the Sabbath day he went into the synagogue, as was his custom. And he stood up to read. The scroll of the prophet Isaiah was handed to him. Unrolling it, he found the place where it is written:

"The Spirit of the Lord is on me,
because he has anointed me
to preach good news to the poor.
He has sent me to proclaim freedom for the prisoners
and recovery of sight for the blind,
to release the oppressed,
to proclaim the year of the Lord's favor."

Then he rolled up the scroll, gave it back to the attendant and sat down. The eyes of everyone in the synagogue were fastened on him, and he began by saying to them, "Today this scripture is fulfilled in your hearing."

All spoke well of him and were amazed at the gracious words that came from his lips. "Isn't this Joseph's son?" they asked.

Jesus said to them, "Surely you will quote this proverb to me: 'Physician, heal yourself! Do here in your hometown what we have heard that you did in Capernaum.'"

"I tell you the truth," he continued, "no prophet is accepted in his hometown. I assure you that there were many widows in Israel in Elijah's time, when the sky was shut for three and a half years and there was a severe famine throughout the land. Yet Elijah was not sent to any of them, but to a widow in Zarephath in the region of Sidon. And there were many in Israel with leprosy in the time of Elisha the prophet, yet not one of them was cleansed—only Naaman the Syrian."

All the people in the synagogue were furious when they heard this. They got up, drove him out of the town and took him to the brow of the hill on which the town was built, in order to throw him down the cliff. (Luke 4:16–29 NIV)

The novelty of Jesus departing from the predictable patterns of the accepted oral traditions was met with rigorous objection. There is a difference between being rigorous and being in a state of rigor mortis, which is a medical term describing the stiffness of the muscular and skeletal systems after death. The word *rigorous* communicates intensity in temperament or action, while the word *rigor mortis* describes the body's immobility because there is no life. We should find ourselves being rigorous for the gospel of Jesus Christ without going to the extreme of losing our ability to respond and react.

The most significant negative implication of the idol of novelty is that it puts one on a path of perpetual searching—not for God but for the next program or idea. This perpetual searching is the perpetual hunger that cannot be satisfied. This is quite contrary to Jesus's teaching that "Blessed are those who hunger and thirst for righteousness, for they will be filled," which ideologically is about contentment and satisfaction (Matt. 5:6 NIV). The perpetual hunger for newness can be identified by symptomatic language. Some of the symptomatic language will include versions of the following: "This is the best program we have ever seen," "You have never seen anything like this before," and "This is the first time we have ever done this".

These versions will also be accompanied by words that invoke God's presence and anticipate what God is about to do. For example, when lured to worship the idol of novelty, we might say, "God is about to do something he has never done before." The reality is that we have become so enamored with our own world that we shape God to fit into it. We just can't imagine a God that would pour out grace upon something that isn't totally new and fabulous. We forget that God's greatest moment of success was lived out on the lonely hill of Golgotha, and that the world's definition of that moment was defeat and death.

The challenge is to identify the presence of God in something that is novel or new without making God subversive to the newness. It may be new to us and new to our experience, but the focus should not be on the newness of something—it should be on what God can do when we use something to build upon what is present.

When the challenge of something new is threatening to us, we make it an evil by shrouding the idea with threats of no longer participating, dreaming up ideas of how many people would leave if we thought of doing something different, and hiding behind barriers of negative conclusions. We kneel at the altar of evil when the new idea doesn't challenge our faith to go deeper into Christ and possibly bring change to the world that we readily enjoy controlling.

As a pastor, I have seen both promising ideas fulfilled, against my better judgment, and have officiated at the funeral of too many novel ideas that were killed before they could be of any influence (even in discussion).

A PARADOX OF NOVELTY

I experienced the paradox of novelty most clearly in my life when our family moved to Allen, Texas, in 1995. I was appointed to start a new United Methodist church to serve the growing area of Collin County in West Allen. My appointment to start a new church is what some people today call a parachute drop. We had no sponsoring congregation, but we did have a parsonage, two other families, and God's faithfulness.

A novel idea at the time was for denominations to identify a pastor, give him compensation, and drop him in an area. The pastor would then gather people and rent a storefront, movie theatre, clubhouse, school, or some other facility as the congregation grew. The congregation would then buy land and eventually build the church. There was only one problem with this plan. It worked when you had developed areas with vacant storefronts, established businesses, or schools. We had none of these, except for a school that was being built.

While many well-intentioned Christian people were threatened by the idea of a new church, three laypeople were not—Glenn, Chuck, and John—a school board president and two school board members who belonged to First United Methodist Church of Allen, Texas. Through a series of discussions, we discovered that the only real obstacle to starting our church in the school was the issue of land. If a church had land, it could rent the school for three years. We had no land, but God had a plan.

There were only two options for land. One was very workable, but the ideal location was land on the south side of McDermott Road. We were told that there was *no way* that the owner would sell, and besides, the purchase would have to be the entire twenty-four acres. Such a purchase would make the acquisition the largest church start land purchase to date in the history of the North Texas Conference of The United Methodist Church. However, the land was already platted with a road that divided the land into two 12-acre parcels. One layman, Sherwood, was not intimidated by the idea of purchasing the entire acreage and then selling twelve acres to reduce the debt.

Today, the result of four laymen not being repulsed by the idea of a new church and not kneeling at the altar of "we've never done it that way before" is now Suncreek United Methodist Church (www.suncreekumc.org). If the dream of a new church had stopped with the reluctance of the vocal, established church members, the dream would have died—but it did not. Others picked up on the dream of something new, undeterred by the novelty of acquisition, and allowed God to bring a new church community into being.

We shouldn't lose sight of the importance of novelty or newness. The words of the prophet Jeremiah (31:31 NIV) tell us, "I [God] will make a new covenant." Jesus's declaration in John 13:34 speaks of new commandments, and in Luke 22:20, he says, "This cup is the new covenant in my blood" (NIV). Paul later tells us "if anyone is in Christ, he is a new creation" (2 Corinthians 5:17 NIV). John shares his vision, "Behold, I [God] make all things new" (Revelation 21:5 KJV). We find that the biblical witness is filled with newness. The word *new, kainos* (Greek) and *chadash* (Hebrew), appears 150 times in the Bible, but it is always as an adjective. It points to something other than itself. Novelty becomes an idol when it does not point toward something greater than itself.

Chapter 2

STRUCTURE

When the only tool you have is a hammer,
then everything looks like a nail.

Structure becomes an idol when we believe that the right organizational structure will alleviate our struggle and fight our battles for us. Our focus and energy are placed on a certain model of ministry or organization so that they become our salvation for the future. The result is that instead of creatively addressing particular needs and responses to indigenous issues and challenges, we replace this with a warehouse wholesale club approach, focusing on specific, prepackaged products and high volume.

The idolatry of structure brings duplication and imitation. Some local congregations and pastors work toward the large church model. These large church models are represented by churches like Willowcreek, Gingamsburg, Church of the Resurrection, and Saddleback. By hosting conferences and seminars on a variety of issues, these large churches are seeking to support the principal work of the kingdom of God; however, when the participant or hosting church focuses on simply duplicating what another large church is doing, it's misled into believing that duplicating this ministry will help it fight the battles that its individuals are facing.

In 1994, I was pastor of Nocona United Methodist Church. I had been to a workshop on worship and was so excited to see the multimedia opportunities available. I attended a seminar on introducing multimedia to small membership churches. The model was to put a large TV and VCR on a cart and to place the cart in the front of the sanctuary to be used. We learned all the details: how to set the time, how to put the VCR on pause so the tape would be ready to be play when needed, and how to amplify the sound if we couldn't patch the cable directly into our sound systems. We learned it all.

The following Sunday, I was excited to use a film clip from *Chariots of Fire*. I paused the tape where I needed it, got the microphone in place, and was ready for worship. My first clue that this probably wouldn't work in Nocona like the workshop model occurred before worship. I left the sanctuary, and someone thought the youth or some other group left the TV and VCR cart in the sanctuary, so he unplugged everything and moved it to the education wing. When I found out, I returned the TV and VCR cart to the sanctuary. I will regret that action for the remainder of my ministry.

There are many reasons why bringing a TV and VCR on a cart into the sanctuary did not work in Nocona. What worked in the seminar in a small room did not work in a large sanctuary. People could neither see nor hear the TV in that large space. What I did learn was that just because it works in a seminar doesn't mean it will work everywhere else. I realized that I forgot to include the people and my context of ministry when thinking about the use of the TV and VCR. Both the people and the context are necessary ingredients when considering if you should do what others are doing. The idolatry of structural imitation comes when we place a high priority on imitating the structure that works for someone else or some other organization, so much so, we cannot adapt what we have learned to our own context.

Throughout the years, I have learned that no matter how admirable another person's life is, my life is not their life. For example, I want to be a healthier person, but I am not a runner nor a swimmer. I've tried running and swimming, but they don't work for me. When I paid for a personal health analysis and metabolic study, I discovered that intermediate training and resistance bands are what would help me achieve my best health. When I go to the gym I don't grab the heaviest dumbbell I can lift. I have learned that this will not help me. If I want to achieve maximum health, I cannot imitate anybody else.

The same is true of churches. I have seen churches struggle, looking for hope in structural imitation, which requires a lot of energy but produces little results. We see a particular church's success, a popular author's idea, or a consultant's recommendation, and we fail to ask how that particular methodology should be adapted and integrated into our church's particular context. We forget that the church is a blend of coercive authority (church paid staff) and persuasive influence (volunteer involvement).

We often hear of large church seminars and workshops that offer all kinds of valuable information on ministry, but we don't acknowledge the impact of a ministry as being relative data. For example, you probably have never heard of Nocona UMC's Jeans and Boots ministry, but relative to context, I believe what that church, in a town of 2,100 people and a county of 17,000 people, has done is as remarkable as any other ministry in a large church setting. The people of Nocona UMC don't carry out this annual ministry because some other large church was offering it as a model. They do this because of who they are.

What do they do? Every December, the church adopts those children in the elementary school whose Christmas will be very meager. In December of 1993 and 1994, that number was nearly one-third of the entire elementary school. The church provides volunteers, and the school district provides the bus. The bus takes the kids seventeen miles to the Walmart in Bowie. Upon arriving, each child gets to choose a pair of shoes and a pair of jeans. The child's name is placed on both, and the women from UMC gift wrap each child's shoes and jeans. Then the gifts are delivered to the school, and the children get to take them home the last day before Christmas break. You could say that Nocona UMC knows their community and how to respond its needs.

A vignette from the life of David best illustrates how not to bow to the idol of structure.

> David said to Saul, "Let no one lose heart on account of this Philistine; your servant will go and fight him." Saul replied, "You are not able to go out against this Philistine and fight him; you are only a boy, and he has been a fighting man from his youth." But David said to Saul, "Your servant has been keeping his father's sheep. When a lion or a bear came and carried off a sheep from the flock, I went after it, struck it and rescued the sheep from its mouth. When it turned on me, I seized it by its hair, struck it and killed it. Your servant has killed both the lion and the bear; this uncircumcised Philistine will be like one of them, because he has defied the armies of the living

God. The LORD who delivered me from the paw of the lion and the paw of the bear will deliver me from the hand of this Philistine." Saul said to David, "Go, and the LORD be with you." Then Saul dressed David in his own tunic. He put a coat of armor on him and a bronze helmet on his head. David fastened on his sword over the tunic and tried walking around, because he was not used to them. "I cannot go in these," he said to Saul, "because I am not used to them." So he took them off. Then he took his staff in his hand, chose five smooth stones from the stream, put them in the pouch of his shepherd's bag and, with his sling in his hand, approached the Philistine." (1 Sam. 17:32–40 NIV)

Saul clearly believes that what David needs to fight Goliath is the same structure he uses (Saul's tunic, coat of armor, helmet, and sword), but David knows that he cannot face the challenge in someone else's armor. David faces Goliath with his sling and his stone—the very staple of every shepherd. If you read the entire account of David found in 1 Samuel, you will notice that he is anointed as the future king before this event but is sent back to the fields to care for the sheep. God was preparing David the shepherd to become David the giant slayer.

The late Bishop Ben Oliphint once said that the only clergy who get into trouble in the ministry—whatever it is—are the ones who forget who they are. David didn't forget, and he knew that he could not face a giant challenge by trying to be someone he was not. David had to be himself.

If we can clearly discern who we are as individuals and communities of faith, then we can look at other structures with a healthy perspective. That perspective seeks to inquire, probe, and discover so it can gain more self-awareness and not to replace who we are. If another structure can help you find and express who you are, then it is probably healthy to implement. If you are envious of another's results and simply jettison your own identity to imitate or duplicate another, then you're probably worshipping the idol of structure.

Chapter 3

DESTINATION

Changing your zip code is not the same
as addressing your problems

The idol of destination is the belief that when we arrive at a particular place, we won't have any more battles to fight or challenges in life. This is a misguided focus on an elusive point that does not exist in reality and robs us of learning how to journey through life.

When we believe that arriving at a particular place will alleviate our need to journey through life, our faith becomes dormant. We never become content, because we are perpetually looking for the next place and are not aware of our current context. When our focus is always on the future, we may miss some valuable information in the present and repeat behaviors and mistakes that we have made in the past. We worship the idol of destination when we see our true fulfillment in life as only coming when we arrive at our next destination.

What we have lost is the art of being content with where we are and what we have. We are no longer able to enjoy life in the moment. If we allow the next destination to define our self-worth and world, we slip into a fog of self-perception and are unable to see into our own soul or out into the world. The key element is for us to find a way to be fully in the moment. As Christians, we must realize that centering our lives in Christ is to discover the sacred tension that exists between being content with where we are while still hungering to become the not-yet that God is developing.

Paul was aware of this tension.

> I am not saying this because I am in need, for I have learned to be content whatever the circumstances. I know what it is to be in need, and I know what it is to have plenty. I have learned the secret of being content in any and every situation, whether well fed or hungry, whether living in plenty or in want. I can do everything through him who gives me strength. (Phil. 4:11–13 NIV)

It is this sense of being content that allows us to be more aware of God in the moment. When we are in this place, our sense of God's presence is heightened in our lives. Maybe the best biblical character to illustrate how to never bow at the altar of destination is Joseph. The record of Joseph's life is found in Genesis, chapters 37 through 50. Joseph was betrayed by his brothers and left for dead, was lied to and lied about, worked from the position of slave to authority and had it all stripped away because of a lie, worked his way back up to a position of authority, and then provided exile for those same brothers who had left him for dead years earlier. Joseph's character is revealed in three short verses.

> Joseph's brothers then came and threw themselves down before him. "We are your slaves," they said.

> But Joseph said to them, "Don't be afraid. Am I
> in the place of God? You intended to harm me,
> but God intended it for good to accomplish what
> is now being done, the saving of many lives. So
> then, don't be afraid. I will provide for you and
> your children." And he reassured them and spoke
> kindly to them. (Gen. 50:20–21 NIV)

Joseph was not waiting for the next destination so that he could find contentment. If he had, his life would have been filled with resentment. Wherever he was, whether at the bottom of a well or in the dungeons, Joseph focused on the journey.

We learn from Joseph's life how not to worship the idol of destination. When we journey like Joseph, we learn to see the sacred that exists in the simple and the holy that abides in the ordinary. We lose our sense of contentment in life when we worship the idol of destination. This is not the same thing as surrendering our dreams. It is the art of allowing our desire for God's presence to grow in our lives regardless of the circumstances. We know that we have "settled" in life when we lose the desire to grow and to be God's instrument within the body of Christ. A content person can recognize the invitation of the Holy Spirit. That person will either accept a new challenge from the Holy Spirit and grow or will stay focused in his current context and reflect on God's design and desire for his life. Contentment is our ability to accept where we are while blessing others by being faithful to who we are, where we are.

Paul knew the importance of this contentment and didn't look for happiness in the next destination. We are most tempted to worship the idol of destination when we believe that it will bring more possessions to us. In his instructions to Timothy, Paul makes this very clear.

> But godliness with contentment is great gain. For we brought nothing into the world, and we can take nothing out of it. But if we have food and clothing, we will be content with that.
>
> *People who want (emphasis mine)* to get rich fall into temptation and a trap and into many foolish and harmful desires that plunge men into ruin and destruction. For the love of money is a root of all kinds of evil. Some people, eager for money, have wandered from the faith and pierced themselves with many griefs. (1 Tim. 6:6–10 NIV)

Paul's instructions here deal clearly with the issue of material possessions and wealth, but we can also insert many other things that do not lead to contentment but to grief. Anything that the world around us would define as success can be placed into this text. People who want to be a certain body type; or people who want a particular car; or people who want a certain position in the company; or people who want to be seen by others as successful are examples of how we can fall into the temptation and trap of believing that a particular destination will end the search for contentment in life. For the Christian, there is but one destination that we should focus on—Heaven. Everything else is in the journey.

I feel the idol of destination can sometimes be found in the debate between traditional and contemporary worship styles in churches. Though no label of worship is conclusive, when worship styles become a conflict instead of a conversation, it is because each side of discussion is fairly clear about these labels.

Dean Gregory L. Jones of Duke Divinity School has said that "tradition is the living faith of the dead and traditionalism is the dead faith of the living". Throughout the church's history, the way we worship has changed to adapt to our world. The creation of the printing press, which made the biblical text available to the common people, was a change the church resisted. What we know as the chancel choir, today, was once a contemporary idea. The congregational singing of hymns caused conflict when it began as well.

The debate around traditional and contemporary worship expresses two different styles that define a particular destination. Those who prefer traditional worship and choirs generally feel that contemporary worship and music are trivial and repetitive. Those who favor contemporary worship generally regard traditional elements of worship as stifling and predictable. Those supporting a particular expression of worship have arrived at a particular destination. Without intentional dialogue, the divisiveness will be deep.

We express this idolatry of destination when we become so focused upon arriving at a particular place, we cannot find the joy of contentment. The motivation for this, both individually and corporately, derives from an attitude that we lack something when compared to others, rather than finding contentment where we are.

In the closing scene of the movie *Bagger Vance*, Hardy Greaves, played by Jack Lemmon, apparently has died. He reflects on life and golf. He says, "Like Bagger said. It's not a game that can be won, only played. So, I play on. I play for the moments yet to come, looking for my place in the field."

So if you haven't found contentment where you are, changing your zip code will not help you find it. Can you live like Joseph and be content like Paul?

Chapter 4

ANSWERS

Judge a man by his questions,
rather than his answers.
(Voltaire)

We live in a "Google it" age. If you have a question, simply type it into the browser on your phone, tablet, or computer, and, immediately, you receive literally thousands of answers. Your Internet browser is even smart enough to correct any misspelled words. In other words, if you can get somewhat close to the spelling of the topic you are searching for, the browser can correct your spelling and find your topic. There are a multitude of effects that come from this search and done approach in our lives. We want immediate answers, now. We have a tendency to accept the information we find on the Internet or read on social media as always being correct. As one social media post said, "You can't trust everything you read on the internet!—Benjamin Franklin."

Most importantly, we lose the wonder of questions. I am not suggesting that we don't need answers. The scientific world presents questions about air quality, water quality, and health diagnosis. The answers to these questions are absolutely important for life. Answers are important, but an answer that is given before a question is even asked can become an idol. This is because it is a patent phrase that is disengaging and is without context. Too often in our faith, we have a tendency to "answer before the question is asked."

In some ways, this rush to answer and the need for immediate answers are seen in the American culture's prescription addictions. Prescription drugs are essential and life-giving to many people, but there are also many times when a patient wants a pill to fix a problem that patient has created by his or her lifestyle and health choices. Downstream medicine treats the symptoms; upstream medicine treats the root cause of the medical condition. When we try to apply answers without a context, we are reacting to symptoms. When we value questions, we are exploring the context of the issue, and questions will lead us to faithful answers.

There are over five thousand questions in the Bible—questions from God, Jesus, and people who were struggling with faith and trying to understand faithfulness. The first question recorded in the Bible is from the serpent, "Now the serpent was more crafty than any of the wild animals the LORD God had made. He said to the woman, 'Did God really say, "You must not eat from any tree in the garden?"'" (Gen. 3:1 NIV). The second question recorded in scripture is from God: "But the LORD God called to the man, 'Where are you?'" (Gen. 3:9 NIV). The struggle of all humanity is found in how we choose to responds to these two primary questions – "Did God really say that?" and "Where are you?". The importance is found in who we answer to—the one who wants to take life or the one who wants to give life. But the power is found in the question and not the answer.

Jesus constantly answered questions by asking questions. In the Gospels, the people asked Jesus 183 questions, but he asked 307 questions. Jesus believed in the power of questions to draw us into deeper intimacy with him and each other. Here are some of the questions Jesus asked. You may want to take time to think about them today:

- If you love those who love you, what reward will you get? (Matt. 5:46)
- If you greet only your own people, how are you doing more than others? (Matt. 5:47)
- Who of you by worrying can add a single hour to your life? (Matt. 6:27)
- Who is your mother, and who are your brothers? (Matt. 12:48)
- What good will it be for a person if he gains the whole world, yet forfeits his soul? Or what can a person give in exchange for his soul? (Matt. 16:26)
- What do you think? If a man owns a hundred sheep, and one of them wanders away, will he not leave the ninety-nine on the hills and go to look for the one that wandered off? (Matt. 18:12)
- What is it you want? (Matt. 20:21)
- Do you bring in a lamp to put it under a bowl or a bed? Instead, don't you put it on its stand? (Mark 4:21)
- What shall we say the kingdom of God is like, or what parable shall we use to describe it? (Mark 4:30)
- Don't you see that nothing that enters a man from the outside can make him "unclean"? (Mark 7:18)
- What do you want me to do for you? (Mark 10:51)

- Which of these three do you think was a neighbor to the man who fell into the hands of robbers? (Luke 10:36)
- So if you have not been trustworthy in handling worldly wealth, who will trust you with true riches? (Luke 16:11)
- For who is greater, the one who is at the table or the one who serves? (Luke 22:27)
- Do you understand what I have done for you? (John 13:12)
- Don't you know me, even after I have been among you such a long time? (John 14:9)
- Who is it you are looking for? (John 20:15)
- Do you love me? (John 21:17)

When a question is a noun, it is defined as "a thing said, written, or done to deal with or as a reaction to a question, statement, or situation." When a question is a verb, it is defined as "a reaction to someone or something." Could it be that we kneel before the altar of answers when we believe having the right information will fight our battles for us? We can see this dynamic in the way people acted and reacted to Jesus's teachings.

There are very few questions left in our informational world today. I suggest that the "caller ID effect" has infiltrated most parts of our lives. With caller ID, we know who is calling before answering the call. We make a large assumption when we think we know that person based on his or her social media posts—the causes that are important to them and the news outlets they listen to or read. In too many ways, we think we know what other peoples' motives and opinions are, when they are really our own shrouded accusations. We see this most clearly in the enormous chasms created between people because of their opinions about political and social issues. But when a natural disaster strikes a community, the divisive opinions that separate us are not important any longer. We have an equally enormous capacity to help each other or to hurt each other.

While I was in Houston, I met regularly with a group of clergy that were not all like-minded. The group confronted my assumptions and broadened my perception of the world. Through our conversations and meals, we discovered that we did have much in common. During the course of the conversations, we would ask each other a question, "What is it in me that is causing me to respond to this issue the way that I am." I carry this question with me daily to guide my self-reflection. When we feel the need to answer a question about a situation or event, maybe it would be good to ask ourselves this question before speaking or acting, "Why do I need to answer this?"

John Maxwell said, "When we are talking we are not learning anything about others; but when we are listening we are learning." There are times when we need an answer, but there are also times when a question might enable us to make a better decision or to learn more. Questions can often tell us more than answers ever will. Wisdom and maturity is to know the balance between asking and telling.

When our son was in the first grade, he asked my wife and me a question, "Mom, Dad, what is sex?" I don't know if any parent is ready for that question. In my mind, I prepared for a lengthy conversation about "the birds and the bees." As I was wondering where to start my lecture, my wife asked, "Micah, why are you asking that question?" Micah replied, "Well, on this form for school it says 'sex'; then M or F." If my wife had not been wise enough to ask her question, our son would have received an answer to a question that he did not ask.

"May I ask you why you are asking that question?" is an opportunity to reengage and listen. Maybe what you are assuming and what is being asked is entirely different. Maybe what is going on in your life has caused you to hear something that isn't being asked. Maybe you only heard part of what is being said or you don't understand. Take a break from immediately giving an answer. Ask another question.

Chapter 5

DEFINING YOUR DASH

Your life is made up of two dates and a dash.
Make the most of the dash.

How do you choose where to kneel? How do you identify what is most important to you and not live a life of regrets?

I have been a pastor for nearly thirty years and have had the sacred honor of being with people in all stages of their lives, but it is the journey at the end of their lives that has had the most lasting impact on me. Sometimes the end of a person's life is the culmination of many years, and death is a welcomed friend that ushers one into eternal life with God. Sometimes the end of life is an unwelcomed enemy, which is stealing time away from that person in a medical diagnosis or tragedy. In any case, what I have come to realize is that none of us is in control of the date of our birth and none of us will be able to avoid the date of our death, but we can define how we live the "dash" between the date of our birth and death. Your life is made of up two dates and a dash, so make the most of your dash.

The first step in "Defining Your Dash" is to do the personal work of defining. The second step is to ask and assess. The third step is to strategize. The final step is to establish habits of the head and heart. In short, your dash is how you:

Define where you are
Assess what you need to change
Strategize to make those changes
Establish chosen **H**abits of the head and heart

Who you are today can be defined as a combination of many factors, but most physiological concepts will revolve around what you believe about your identity. There are entire psychological disciplines dedicated to the exploration of self-understanding. For the sake of our defining work, I would like to focus on two concepts.

First, there is the definition of identity. The *Oxford Dictionary* defines identity as, "The fact of being who or what a person or thing is." Secondly, I believe that Hazel Rose Markus summarizes what contributes to our identities as she discusses the clash between independence and interdependence in her book, Clash! 8 Cultural Conflicts That Make Us Who We Are. She states, "All of us have two sides to ourselves: an *independent* side that wants to be separate, unique, and in control; and an *interdependent* that wants to be connected, similar, and cooperative."

I suggest that most of our identities are living in a less-conscious reactivity to this dynamic in our lives. The independent and interdependent dynamics become a jumbled mess of experiences that shape our identities. We see this in the cycles of human relationships that are repeated. Left unexplored, these "cycles" of human behavior can be seen at least in the cycles of poverty and the cycles of abuse. I can remember answering the phone at my parents' house. The caller started a conversation with me because my voice sounded just like my father's. What I want to suggest is that our identities have less to do with our DNA and more to do with our inherited behaviors.

To define your identity, you need to explore who you are. Write your own biography because it will help you understand what contributes to your identity.

The following exercise will help you write your own life story or memoir. There is a list of suggestions and questions that will guide you as you get started. Don't limit your writing to only answering the questions but rather let them guide you. After you have completed your writing, look for patterns and insights to help you define what people, experiences, and dynamics contribute to your identity.

> Where were you born?
>
> What do you know of your ancestors (grandparents, aunts, uncles, etc.)?
>
> What do you know of your parents' histories (or those persons who raised you)?
>
> How many brothers and sisters do you have?
>
> What do you remember about your childhood home? Did your family move when you were a child?
>
> What memories do you have about your childhood? Include the good and the bad ones.
>
> What do you remember about your primary school years?
>
> What did you want to be when you were a child? Why?

What was life like at home (holidays, dinners, family trips, and day-to-day life)?

As you think about your home life, what do you remember fondly? What painful memories do you have of this time? Was there a particular traumatic or dramatic event that changed your life?

How did you relate to your siblings?

Who were the most significant people in your life? Why?

What were your junior high school and senior high school years like?

What are the events and experiences that brought you joy?

What events brought you sadness? Why?

How did you see conflict handled in your family?

What traits, habits, and behaviors from each of your parents did you inherit?

Using two to five year increments, write about the people and life experiences that made the biggest impact in your life.

How is your occupation similar or different from your siblings' occupations?

How is your relationship similar or different from your siblings' relationships to your parents?

Now, we begin the work of Assessing. To assess is to "evaluate or estimate the nature, ability, or quality of." As you reflect on your writing, ask yourself:

When did I express my "independence" (the need to be unique)?

When did I express my "interdependence" (the need to be similar or meet expectations of others)? Where are those choices of my independence and interdependence still being expressed today?

Let me share some experiences from my own life assessment that demonstrate how my identity today was shaped by experiences in life. The first experience took place when I was ten years old. I am the third child in my family. My two sisters are nine and ten years older than I am. Because my parents were more established in their careers, I was given extraordinary opportunities that not everyone gets to have. I was given the chance to float down a tributary of the Amazon River in Bolivia, with my parents, after they led a missions group for twenty-one days in the jungles of Bolivia. At the age of eleven, I accompanied my mother on a medical mission to Africa. During my high school years, I attended Wichita Falls High School and was able to participate in any sport or extracurricular activity I wanted to. I worked at the church where my father was a Pastor and my supervisor was Oscar Pope, who had less formal education than me but taught me things that I wasn't aware I did not know. Skin color didn't matter in our home. We had missionaries from all over the world staying at our home at one time or another. Even before I was born, our family had been very close to a man who became an instrumental leader, pastor and eventually a bishop of The United Methodist Church in Bolivia. These are some of the experiences and the varieties of cultures that I was introduced to. And these are just a few of the reasons that I am passionate about missions outreach in the churches that I serve.

In April 1979, a devastating tornado hit Wichita Falls, Texas. My dad was instrumental in the relief work on many levels. His passion for the needs of people led him to be the leader of a community group which created The Wichita Falls Food Bank. My dad believed that the work of providing food for people, whose homes were destroyed, shouldn't stop after the summer work camps of 1979 concluded.

In 2008, I was the pastor of Bear Creek United Methodist Church in Houston, Texas. Our church was a Red Cross shelter for nearly a month. For thirteen days we had no electricity. The response of the people in our community was amazing. Regardless of the church affiliation, church people were taking laundry home for people in the shelter and returning clothes clean and folded. Every night a different church group would bring homemade food and desserts. Our church converted a group of computers into a computer lab to help families with their FEMA applications. From that experience I realized that our church must respond to the needs of our community in more practical ways. Within a year, we had created The Houston Northwest Community Center, which Bear Creek United Methodist then operated. Though I was not conscious of it at the time, what I had seen in my father's attitude was imbedded in my spirit.

Not everything that you are doing today is productive and healthy. As you assess your story, you'll discover something about your identity. Some things should be celebrated while others need to change. The final step of assessing is both simplistic and difficult.

Make a list of the things that you want to change or do differently in life. Then identify the historic connection to that issue in your life. The best way to do this is to take a piece of paper and draw a line down the middle of the page. On the left side, write down the issue or thing you want to change. On the right side, write the historic connection you can make to that issue in your life story. Here is an example of how this exercise might look:

Issues or Areas I Want to Change	Personal History Connection
I want to criticize people less. I always seem to find myself pointing out the faults of family, friends, and the people with whom I work.	In our home growing up, I remember hearing criticisms on a regular basis. It wasn't always directed at me, but even when I did something I thought was good, only the bad things were pointed out. If I got a 90 percent on a test, I was asked why it wasn't a 95 percent. Dinner discussions seemed to involve a lot of conversations that criticized people we knew in our family, neighborhood, church, and community. Our family seemed to be really good at finding what we thought was wrong with others.

This exercise may also include the lingering phrases and messages that are a part of your psyche and are connected to your personal history. Hearing words like "Who do you think you are? You can't do that?" often have a significant influence on our adult identity. Sometimes we are consciously aware of these messages. Sometimes they are subtle messages that inform our identities.

What are the things you want to change? How do you understand those things as being related to your personal history? Understanding the connections between your history and your actions today is critical.

Now you are ready to take the next step of Strategizing. A strategy is "a plan of action designed to achieve a long-term or overall aim." Strategizing is intentionally using the "ing" tense of the verb to suggest that this work is an ongoing process.

Get a piece of paper, and at the top of the page, write down one issue in your life that you want to focus on changing. As you did in your assessing work, draw a line down the middle of the page. On the left side write the words "What I CAN control." On the right side, write the words "What I CAN NOT control." Here is an example of how this exercise might look:

I want to criticize people less

What I CAN control	What I CAN NOT control
My thoughts	Situations
The words I use	Circumstances
When I choose to talk or respond	Others ideas, opinions, or words
My attitude	What others think or feel about me
Offering my opinion when not asked	
How I answer questions	
What I think and feel about myself	

This exercise will also help you strategize how to approach specific situations. The key is to recognize what is not in your control and what is in your control. Regardless of the situation, this strategic approach will help you to focus your energy and your thoughts. Too often, we waste energy focusing on the things that are beyond our control.

Here are some things I have discovered about how and why we make changes in our lives at this stage:

- Change happens in our lives when the pain of staying the same becomes greater than the pain of changing
- We have a tendency to react more than to respond, and those reactions are based on our identities and our needs
- When faced with the awareness that we need to make a change, we will focus most of our energy on what produces the least amount of change
- Changing what is in our control and what matters the most is often the hardest work for us to do
- When we consider what needs to change, it is best to remember that we choose our actions but cannot choose the consequences
- The most difficult and important work for change is the work I need to do

Now you are ready to address the Habits of the head and heart. This personal work revolves around one central thought, *You are not what you say, but you are what you do.*

A habit is a permanent pattern of behavior that allows you to navigate life. When you first learn how to type, to tie your shoe, or to drive a car; it's hard work. There are so many little steps to remember. But after you learn, it becomes habitual. This means it is quite literally "in your body" (or muscle memory). Neurologists call the process where the brain converts a sequence of actions into routine activity, "chunking." Habits are not only found in our physical actions. We have habits of the head and heart.

Habits of the head are those thoughts that are "chunked" into how you most immediately respond to situations and circumstances in life. The habits of the head are the cognitive processes that define the differences between an optimist and a pessimist. Some people see the glass half full while others see the glass half empty.

The habits of the heart are expressed in our emotional reactions to experiences in life. What we think and what we feel are the cumulative effects of our experiences in life.

Putting your strategy into practice will be the key ingredient to reshaping your habits. It has been said that the definition of insanity is doing the same thing over and over again while expecting different results. How does your dash look? If you will take time to define where you are, assess what you need to change, strategize how to make those changes, and establish chosen habits of the head and heart, you will determine your dash.

A Final Word

"So here's what I want you to do, God helping you: Take your everyday, ordinary life—your sleeping, eating, going-to-work, and walking-around life—and place it before God as an offering. Embracing what God does for you is the best thing you can do for him. Don't become so well-adjusted to your culture that you fit into it without even thinking. Instead, fix your attention on God. You'll be changed from the inside out."
(Rom. 12:1–2 MSG)

How much of life is lived without even thinking? We have so much stuff, it often takes something like a tragic accident or a natural disaster to recognize what is most important in life. Families are so busy with activities and personal technological devices that they are now planning "family nights" and setting rules to put down the cell phone. We eat on the go so we can be busy when we arrive. In the midst of this fast-paced world, we can just fit into it without thinking. We let the outside world change us on the inside. We sit on the couch with remote controls and communicate with each other by texting.

But these words from Paul ring as true today as they did some two thousand years ago, "Fix your attention on God. You'll be changed from the inside out" (verses 1–2).

In the movie *Scent of a Woman*, Al Pacino plays the role of a blind, retired Lieutenant Colonel Frank Slade, who develops a friendship with student Charlie Simms, played by Chris O'Donnell. Charlie is in a prep school on a scholarship and may be kicked out of school because of a prank he witnessed on campus involving the dean of the school. During the hearing for disciplinary action, Frank Slade speaks on Charlie's behalf, saying, "I've been around, you know? There was a time I could see. And I have seen. Boys like these, younger than these, their arms torn out, their legs ripped off. But there isn't nothin' like the sight of an amputated spirit. There is no prosthetic for that."

If we expect to live, we cannot avoid the process of life. We are seduced into consumerism by the latest new thing. We think having order in our lives will eliminate our struggles. But the joy of life is not only in the destinations but also in the journey. The wonder of life is not only in the answers but also in the awe. If we will focus on God, pain is redeemed, failures are transformed into new opportunities, and our intentional choices will enable us to celebrate all of life that is the dash between the date of our birth and death. Choose carefully where you kneel.

Printed in the United States
By Bookmasters